# salmonpoetry

*Diverse Voices from Ireland and the World*

MORE PRAISE FOR *The Talking Stick: O Pookering Kosh*

One of the enduring joys of poetry is 'encounter'. As readers, if we are open to it, we can encounter the imaginative world of the poet in all of its rich variety. *The Talking Stick: O Pookering Kosh* by Raine Geoghegan brings the reader into direct contact with Geoghegan's Romani tradition. This is a generous book that does not shy from describing discrimination, bullying, and importantly the child's eye view of encountering her 'difference' in 'the welfare of settled rings' (Allen Fisher, *Dispossession and Cure*). Yet, the reader could never mistake this book for a polemic of confrontation. Geoghegan's "O Pookering Kosh" evinces a sure hand imbued with a deft musicality that sings through each and every page. There is a lightness of touch and generosity in this book. Geoghegan has provided a language glossary at the base of each of the poems in the book.

Our encounter with Geoghegan's tradition is carried in songs like "O Lillai Gillie" and the Romani laying-out tradition unfolds before our eyes in the beautiful "A song to rest the tired dead'. In our century of movement and 'not-at-homeness' caused by wars, climate change and by human desperation, we are confronted with the importance of the stories that we tell and how they are carried from place to place. Geoghegan's "The Gypsy Camp at Auschwitz" is a stunning exposition of human cruelty and survival at the most desperate time in our human history, her handling of this theme is both visually arresting and tonally perfect. Geoghegan's work demonstrates an embodiment of remembrance. When I first published Raine Geoghegan's work, I was taken by the sound and rhythm of the song "O Lillai Gillie". It truly delights me that her work will reach a wider audience.

**Chris Murray**
Poet, Founder of Poethead and Curator of Fired,
an archive for Irish women Poets and the Canon (2017-2019)

*Happy Birthday dear Howie*

# The Talking Stick

*O Pookering Kosh*

*Poems by*

## Raine Geoghegan

*many blessings on your path*

*Love, Light & Beauty*

*Raine Simon*
*x*

*31 August, 2024*

Published in 2022 by
Salmon Poetry
Cliffs of Moher, County Clare, Ireland
Website: www.salmonpoetry.com
Email: info@salmonpoetry.com

Copyright © Raine Geoghegan, 2022

ISBN 978-1-915022-15-8

All rights reserved. No part of this publication may be reproduced or transmitted in any form or by any means, electronic or mechanical, including photography, recording, or any information storage or retrieval system, without permission in writing from the publisher. The book is sold subject to the condition that it shall not, by way of trade or otherwise, be lent, resold or otherwise circulated without the publisher's prior consent in any form of binding or cover other than that in which it is published and without a similar condition, including this condition, being imposed on the subsequent purchaser.

Cover & Title Page Image:
*Raine Geoghegan*

Cover Design & Typesetting: *Siobhán Hutson*

*Printed in Ireland by Sprint Print*

*Salmon Poetry gratefully acknowledges the support of*
*The Arts Council / An Chomhairle Ealaíon*

'The time of the wandering Gypsies has passed.
But I see them, they are bright,
Strong and clear like water.'

BRONISLAWA WAJS
known as Papusza
Romani Poet
(17.08.08 – 8.02.87)


'Can you rocker Romani?
Can you poove a grai?
Can you chore a kanni?
While the mush is jelling by?'

OLD ROMANI SONG

I dedicate this book to my Romany grandmother Amy Lane,
née Ripley, (1912-2005) who walks the path with me.
To my granddaughter Amelia Joan Geoghegan, born in 2021
and to my husband Simon Callow.

# Contents

A Note on the Talking Stick

Although it's not practised any more, it was once a custom in some Romany families that when an elder died, a ritual was performed using the blackthorn stick as a way to pass on wisdom and knowledge from that elder to a small child.

# A Memory of the Hop Fields

She is in the front garden
bending low, picking bluebells,
wearing her old red apron,
with the Spanish dancer on the front.

She stands up, rubbing her lower back,
her mind shaping a memory.
The hop fields,
her mother lean, strong,

picking the hops as quick as a squirrel.
Her bal in plaits, tied on top of her head.
Her gold hoops pulling her ears down.
Ruddy cheeks, dry cracked lips.

Her father pulling poles,
sweating, smiling,
his gold tooth for all to see.

At the end of a long day
she would stand on top of an apple crate,
comb his hair, kiss his neck tasting of salt.

He would pick her up,
Swing her high, low and say,

*'You're the prettiest little chi there ever was.'*

*Bal* – hair; *Chi* - daughter/child.

# they lit fires, moved in close

*dikka kie my carrie come and sit yerself down*

*yer look dukkered*

*me granny used to sit by the yog all the time*
*rubbin 'er 'ands then movin' 'em close to the flames*
*'er skin turned dark and she said that the fire did it*
*dark raddi's with no moon*
*only the brightness of the yog*

*great aunt bethy tellin' a story*
*the one about 'er great great granny margret*
*who drowned in a ditch drunk as a lord*
*'er face down in the water*
*'alf a dozen piglets running around and over 'er,*
*them not seemin' to notice*

*'ands 'oldin' saucers of mesci with drops of tatti-panni in 'em*

*all of the malts slowly gettin' skimmished*

*Dikka kie* – look here; *Dukkered* – done in; *Yog* – fire; *Raddi's* – nights
*Mesci* – tea; *Tatti-panni* – brandy; *Malts* – women; *Skimmished* – drunk

# under a gooseberry bush

*im john ripley*

somewhere in kent, this is where I was borned and laid in me mother's arms, crying for me dear life. it was a warm day in june, me mum and 'er people were on their way to the 'op fields in peasmarsh. me dad 'ad gone ahead to meet some mushes, don't ask. me poor mum was findin' it 'ard, 'er carryin' me near to 'er time and the bump, bump, bump of the wheels of the vardo.

they stopped in the poove to 'ave some 'obben, aunt may was makin' joey gray, the chavies were runnin' around. me mum was soakin' 'er feet in cool water. that's when it started, 'er waters broke and the bowl went flyin', there was 'ollerin' and shoutin', aunt may moved me mum under the bushes, told me cousin to get 'elp from another travelling family. it was touch and go, according to me bein' the wrong way round but thank the lord there was a rackley who 'ad delivered a lot of chavies, she pulled me out and I was borned.

I was named john ripley, after me dad. the 'ead rom came down and blessed me, he tied a little bag of rowan berries round me neck to ward off the bad mulo and to bring kushtie bokt. all the racklies put a little coin in me 'and, as was the custom. luckily me aunt and uncle 'ad left patrin signs along the way so we 'ad plenty of folk to wet me little 'ead. it's not everyday a chavi gets borned under a gooseberry bush. 'course I never 'eard the end of it, me mum and dad teased me rotten and when I tells folks they don't believe it, mind you, it set me up fer life, gave me strength and I've 'ad a bloody kushtie life, I can tell yer. me mum used to tell me this story over and over, to tell yer the truth I've loved tellin' it as much as 'earing it.

*ardo* – wagon; *Poove* – field; *Hobben* – food; *Chavies* – children; *Head Rom* – Gypsy elder; *Racklies* – women; *Patrin* – leaves tied up and left on trees or by the roadside to let families know which way the wagons went.

# The Clearing

*Late Summer 1938*

We used to walk out together on dark nights, to get away from the talk of war. 'Ee called it the 'mothering darkness' and said that nothin' could 'arm us while we were together. I would trip over stumps and stones and 'ee'd tighten 'is grip and say. *'Yer alright me wiv me.'* We talked a lot about each of our dad's, things they said, and their mannerisms. Mine would pretend 'ee was boxin', 'is fists would come up an' 'ee'd lunge at yer. Alf laughed and said 'ee knew a few chal's that used to do that. 'Is dad used to chew on a matchstick then spit it out on the floor, funny 'cause now I look back that's exactly what Alf did once we was married. As the black of the night lifted and the moon sneaked through the clouds, we saw what was in front of us, we saw it clear as day an' when we came to the clearin', I leaned in close, smellin' the fresh scent of soap on 'im and the woody smell of the poove. 'Ee said:

    *'Look at that moon Ame, there ain't nuthin' like it in the 'ole world'*

*Chals* – men; *Poove* – field

# I'm a Travelling Gypsy

A windy day on Hastings beach.
A young lad with thick dark hair
and strong cheek bones kicks his chockas off,
rolls up his trousers and walks along the sand.

He comes to a place where the carriages stop.
    *'I'll catch plenty of guerros and racklies 'ere,*
    *yearn meself a few bob.'*
He places his cap on the sand, clears his throat.

    *Me name's John Ripley, I'm a travelling gypsy.*
    *Dik at me dance, shoon me a gillie.*
    *I'll cheer you up, when the cold wind blows.*
    *It's cold on 'astings beach, don't I know.'*

He takes out his mouth organ, wipes it with his sleeve,
cups it in his vasts then plays an old tune, 'It's a kushti life.'
As he plays, he jogs on one foot then the other, lifting
his knees high, a few spectators, smile, chuckle at him.

By midday his cap is almost full of pennies.
He lays down on his back, looking up at the far sky.
He'd come back tomorrow, slip out of the vardo,
once his dad had gone to feed the grai.

He'd get mullered if the old man found out.
    *'I'll 'ave to be a bit crafty, 'ide me poshes somewhere safe.'*
He drops the coins into his pocket, puts his cap on,
carries his chockas and whistles as he makes his way home.

*Chokkas* – shoes; *Guerros* – men; *Raklies* – women; *Dik* – look; *Shoon* – listen; *Vasts* –
hands; *Kushti* – very good; *Vardo* – wagon; *Grai* – horses; *Mullered* – killed; *Poshes* – money

# great aunt tilda, a funny old malt

me great aunt tilda, now there was a character, a funny old malt. she was me dad's aunt on the lane side of the family. she always wore men's clothes, dark coloured trousers, shirts, waistcoats, a black stadi with a gold 'at pin on the side and a little purple feather. she smoked a swiggler, her fingers yellowed from nicotine. she carried a carpet bag wherever she went, inside a flask of strong black tea with a little drop of panni in it. she'd refuse anyone else's tea, sayin', *'yer never know what they put in it.'* she spoke in a deep voice. when she got in a temper it grew deeper, us gels would be frit to death.

every friday night she'd go the brown bear, 'ave a few drinks with the family, often getting skimmished and if granny amy was there she'd end up fightin' and cursin'. the men would 'ave to pull 'er off me granny, they just couldn't get on, those two. before she went 'ome, she'd shout out. *'i've 'ad enough of this place, I'm goin' 'ome to get a sooti.'* she'd walk all the way 'ome, over seven miles. she never would get on a bus, didn't matter 'ow far she 'ad to go.

when she turned sixty, she packed up 'er covels and went to the care 'ome in shepperton, phil common it was called. we all thought it strange but she said that she didn't want to be a burden on anyone. she still went calling and did 'er little bit of shoppin' but that was 'er 'ome until she died, I think it was some eighteen years later. she'd never married, said she was 'appy without an 'usband. sometimes, she told jokes and rokkered a lot in romani, *'rokker more romanes,'* she'd say.

if someone was ill or grievin', she'd say, *'I'll burn a bit've salt for 'em.'* If someone got in a car or did something adventurous, she'd say *'if yer goes and kills yerself, don't come back and blame me.'* me dad always spoke of 'er but he used to make us laugh when he said, 'our tilda's *a funny old malt, always's 'as been, always's will be.'*

---

*Stadi* – trilby hat; *Panni* – brandy; *Swiggler* – pipe; *Calling* – buying and selling clothes
*Rokkered* – spoke; *Skimmished* – tipsy/drunk; *Malt* – woman; *Sootti* – a good sleep

# Dark is the Forest

Dark is the forest and deep,
In times gone past it's where we'd sleep.
Under the oaks or the Hawthorn tree,
drop our covels, our minds roam free.
Dark is the forest and deep,
for dukkering, our malts will keep,
a small gold ring tied with string,
around their wrist or in their fist.
Dark is the forest and deep,
where foxgloves grow and deer do leap,
our plans are spun and boar will run.
We take our time, we 'ave some fun.
Dark is the forest and deep,
we pass by patrins for those who seek,
to keep in touch with folk that are dear
and pass on news of birth and fear.
Dark is the forest and deep.

Covels – belongings; Dukkering – fortune telling
Patrins – signs left along the way, can be leaves or string

NOTE: The title is taken from the poem "No 131 – Poems 1916" by Edward Thomas.

# Hotchiwitchi

to bake an 'otchiwitchi;
roll it in the clay,
drop it in the embers of yer yog.

go and sing a song,
chase a shushi down the drom,
do a little jig, jog, jog.

when you open up the clay,
the spines will come away,
what's left is sweet and tasty.

chank it while its 'ot,
it maybe all we got,
gadje food it's not

chew yer little jig, jog, jog
chew yer little jig, jog, jog

*Hotchiwitchi / jog jog* — hedgehog;  *Yog* — fire;  *Drom* — road
*Shushi* — rabbit;  *Chank* — eat;  *Gadje* — non-Romany

# To be a Romany

Let me tell yer what it was like to be a Romany in the old days.
We lived in vardo's, made love and fought in 'em.
We picked 'ops, fruit and veg until our backs were sore.
We made pegs and sold 'em along the drom.
Then there were the gillies we sang until our voices were 'oarse.
The boards we laid down in the beer shop so we could step dance.
The 'erbs we picked to mend our body and spirit.
The drabo's passed down.
Tea leaves left in a cup to read.
Cards spread on the table awaiting the dukkerer.
Chavies brought up to rokker the Romani.
We 'elped each other out no matter what.
We cooked on the yog, rabbit stew, hotchiwitchi and Joey Grey.
When one of ours died, we'd sit up all night.
We'd drink mesci or whiskey, sing some of the old songs,
the next day the vardo's and covels were burnt.
There was tottin', raggin', sellin' the loolladi.
We worshipped the ground that we walked on,
the fresh air, green spaces, the lungo drom,
meetin' up with friends, getting' the grai ready for travelling
and finding the next atchin tan.
All this and more.
I'll tell you what it was like to be a Romany in the old days.
It was bloody kushti.

*Vardos* – wagons; *Drom* – road; *Gillies* – songs; *Drabo's* – spells and potions; *Dukkerer* – fortune teller; *Chavies* – children; *Rokker* – speak; *Yog* – fire; *Hotchiwitchi* – hedgehog; *Mesci* – tea; *Covels* – belongings; *Gorgio* – non Romany; *Kushti* – good; *Totting* – dealing in junk/scrap; *Ragging* – selling old clothes; *Loolladi* – flowers; *The Lungo drom* – the long road; *Grai* – horses; *Atchin tan* – stopping place

# Gypsy Lullaby

I'll sing you a lullaby
my wild, Romani chi
then you must sleep
dream of shushi and grai.


I'll sing you a lullaby
my beautiful chi,
I'll cast a draba
how peaceful you'll lie.

*Chi* – small child; *Shushi* – rabbit; *Grai* – horse; *Draba* – spell

# Apple Picking Days in the Vale of Evesham

You're in the orchard,
sitting on the grass
with the woody scent of apples and earth,
a basket full of Worcester Pearmans at your feet.

You take the smallest one,
wipe it on your purple apron,
lean your head back to catch the sun.

    *''ere you are my gel, a kushti slice of apple.'*

        Four years old again and daddy is cutting the fruit,
        slicing it with his special little churi,
        the one his father gave him.
        He grins as the juice dribbles down your chin.

One hand on your belly
you feel the baby kick,
you take another bite,
watch your husband in the tree,
his strong hands pulling the fruit
from the branches
taking one from the right
another from the left
dropping them into the straw basket
which hangs low around his neck

        *'not long to go now.'*

he climbs down the ladder
drops his load onto the soft earth
stretches his arms wide

        *'yer done now, Alf?'*
        *'yes, my love.'*

Fifty years later
as you wave goodbye to your granddaughter,
you remember,
the baby kicking,
Alf in the tree,
autumn sunshine
and the strong smell of the Worcesters.

*Kushti* – very nice; *Churi* – a small knife

# The Way of the Gypsy

Amy took off her coat, untied her money belt, looked at her daughter
who had a hula hoop at her feet.

*'Make me some mesci child and a sandwich,*
*I'm famished and full of dust, jel on.'*

She'd had a good day, had sold all the flowers,
even the dahlias that were past their best.
Her back ached, her pirroes were sore but she was smiling.

She was slowly growing accustomed to the house,
the big rooms, windows that needed cleaning every week.

She wasn't sure about the neighbours,
Especially the one with all the cats,
she seemed to look down her nose at Amy.

She missed the vardo, cooking on the yog
and the open tober.

*'Thank the blessed Lord we're goin' 'oppin,'*
she said under her breath.
Two more weeks and they'd be off to Bishop's Frome
in beautiful Herefordshire.

*Mesci* – tea; *Jel on* – move on; *Pirroes* – feet; *Vardo* – wagon; *Yog* – fire; *Tober* – road

# O Lillai Gillie

*(Angloromani)*

Prey o lillai, prey o lillai
Gillyava a gillie
Prey o chick, prey o charos
Gillyava a gillie

Prey a panni, prey o panni
Gillyava a gillie
Shoon me vas' tacha
Gillyava a gillie

Prey o raddi, prey o raddi
Gillyava a gillie
Chumos for me pen
Gillyava a gillie

Prey o lillai, prey o lillai
Gillyava a gillie
Prey o chick, prey o charos
Gilyava a gillie

Gillyava a gillie, gillyava a gillie
Shoon me vas tatcha,
Gillyava a gillie

# The Summer Song

In the summer, in the summer
I will sing a song
Of the earth, of the heavens
I will sing a song

On the river, on the river
I will sing a song
Listen my beloved
I will sing a song

In the night, in the night
I will sing a song
Kisses for my love
I will sing a song

In the summer, in the summer
I will sing a song
Of the earth, of the heavens
I will sing a song

I will sing a song, a song
Listen my beloved,
I will sing a song

# 'a song to rest the tired dead'

*i.m. of Celia Lane*

it is dusk
she has come to wash the body
a table is set by the bed
a bowl of lavender water
clean muslin cloths
a white towel

   *'too young for death'*

she thinks as she removes all the clothing
and jewellery from the body of her niece
she notices stretch marks on the thighs
how the breasts have dropped
from feeding the chavies

   *'forty years ago, just been borned*
*sucking at her Daya's breast.'*

taking a cloth
she dips it in water
squeezes it hard in her hand
sets about her task

malts stand by the door way
aunts, daughters, sisters and the daya
singing in low soft voices
a song to rest the dead

she speaks quietly
to her loved one as she gently cleans
lifting one arm up then the other
holding it
placing it down carefully
as if it was made of glass

the others won't move too close
it is mokkadi to do so

this woman who washes the dead
now holds both feet
letting them rest for a while
blessing them for all the miles
they have trod the earth

she dresses her niece in the finest of clothes
combs her dark tangled hair
places the gold chain and earrings in the palm
of the right hand
puts the wedding ring back on
the third finger of the left hand

   *such small fingers*

bending forward, kisses them

   *you are ready now my gel, sov well*

*Chavies* – children; *Daya* – mother; *Malts* – women; *Mokkadi* – unclean; *Sov* – sleep

# The Pookering Kosh – The Talking Stick

Me granda is dyin'.
We're packed tight inside the vardo.
*'Dik at the old guerro,'* me cousin says.
'E ain't long fer this world.' Well. We all jin that.
I'm crouching by the door when an ole' mush
comes in carryin' a stick of blackthorn.
*''Ere's the pookering kosh,'* me granny says.
She picks up the youngest, our Emily and puts 'er on the bed.
The ole' mush gives the kosh to me granda, who can barely 'old it.
Me granny takes the chavies vast and squeezes the other end of the
kosh into 'er little fingers.
Everyone is quiet.
The mush sings a gillie, well it's more like diddlin to me.
Me granda lifts 'is 'ead, smiles at Emily then falls back wiv a gasp.
No one moves. I'm 'oldin' me breath.
The chavi takes the kosh and waves it in the air.
Me granny says, 'That's right our gel, we jin what you're doin.'
She laughs then roves, one by one they rove until
they're all at it and I breathe out.
I whispers to me cousin, *'Come on, let's jel and play in the poove.'*
We get out of that vardo quick sharp, we leave 'em to it.

*Vardo* – wagon; *Dik* – look; *Guerro* – man; *Jin* – to know;  *Mush* – man; *Chavi* – child; *Vast* – hand;
*Gillie* – song; *Diddlin* – singing diddiley dees; *Roves* – weeps; *Jel* – come on; *Poove* – field

NOTE: It is the custom in some Romany families that when an elder dies a ritual is practised using
the blackthorn stick as a way to pass on wisdom and knowledge from that elder to a small child.

# Koring Chiriclo I – a triolet

When the Romanies were forced off the roads into houses they were
saddened by the fact that they could no longer hear the cuckoo sing

I've loved to hear the cuckoo sing.
I'm a Romany, always travelling
from Huntingdon to King's Lyn.
I've loved to hear the cuckoo sing
since I was a chavy in a sling.
Summer, autumn, winter spring.
I've loved to hear the cuckoo sing.
I'm a Romany. Always travelling.

*Koring Chiriclo* – a cuckoo. *Chavi* – small child

# Koring Chirclo II – a triolet

Jel on, me dad would say.
Pack up yer covels, we'll be on our way.
Take our time, get to Frome's Hill by May.
Jel on, me dad would say.
The cuckoo's callin', untie the grai,
up onto the vardo. It's a kushti day.
Jel on, me dad would say.
Pack up yer covels. We'll be on our way.

*Koring chiriclo* – the cuckoo; *Jel on* – move on; *Covels* – belongings;
*Grai* – horses; *Vardo* – wagon; *Kushti* – lovely

# On the Tober with Loolladi

Every Friday and Saturday Granny was up early tying bunches of loolladi then putting them on her cart. She wore a paisley scarf, a dark blue money belt with a side pocket round her waist, gold earrings and a gold sovereign on a chain at her neck. I liked to sit on the back doorstep and watch her. She tied them with a string called bass. When it got wet it frayed and smelled of Weetabix. She worked swiftly, rhythmically and when all the flowers were on the cart she stood back, admiring them as if she was looking at a work of art. My favourites were dahlias, deep purples, soft reds, bright orange. I also loved sweet peas. Sometimes Granny would give me one to put on my pillow and I'd fall asleep smelling the lovely scent.

I would open the gate for her, in my pyjamas. The familiar sound of the wheels rolling over the drain in the alleyway made me think of trains.

*'Bye my gel, see to Granfaver, won't yer?'*

*'Alright Granny,'* I'd reply.

On her return in the late afternoon, her cart empty, her face glowing. She'd say,

*'Alf, make me a cup of mesci, I'm parched.'*

While Grandfather was making her tea she would untie the money belt, count out her poshes. I'd kneel on the floor and watch her place the coins and notes in piles. Then she'd say,

*'The Lord's good, but I ain't arf dukkering.'*

Into my hands she'd drop some coins.

*'Right now, let's get the 'obben on.'*

That night we'd have a proper feast, lamb chops, mashed potatoes, ham and piccalilli, carrots and peas, fresh crusty bread or the left over Joey Gray that Grandfather loved. Sometimes we had fresh strawberries from Kent and whipped cream.

When we finished eating, we'd flop on the sofa and armchairs for a while and watch telly. I'd help Granny to wash up. Grandfather, well he'd go for a walk and a smoke, I could smell it on his breath when he kissed me goodnight. Sometimes I would teach Granny a new word, writing it down so she could copy letter for letter. The curtains pulled, doors locked. I would go to bed and fall asleep listening to Grandfather playing a lullaby on his harmonica.

*Tober* — road; *Loolladi* — flowers; *Mesci* — tea; *Dukkering* — aching; *Obben* — dinner

# Aunt Ria's Gypsy Gold

sovereigns and gold chains
hanging from her neck and wrists
rings through ears on fingers

at night
she places them in an embroidered bag
slips it under the mattress

she sleeps soundly
as the gold warms itself
longing for her soft skin
and light

# Keep movin'

The last weekend in May, a Friday, we pulled up on the poove. We got the fire goin' and washed the little chavvies ready for bed. Our Ria and me were drinking mesci when our Sammy shouted. *'Dick-eye the gavvers are comin'.'* All the malts came out of the vados and we stood there. We 'ad to 'old the men back as the gavvers started to wreck the site. One of 'em kicked the kittle off the yog. He shouted, *'Pack up and get going, you're not welcome 'ere.'* I 'ad to 'old my Alfie back, 'e don't lose 'is temper much but when 'e does, watch out, like that time he snoped a guerro in the yock outside the beer shop an' ended up in the cells for a night. It rained 'ard, we got drenched as we packed up all our covels. The chavvies were cryin', the men swearin' under their breath knowin' if they said anythin' they'd get carted off. Our Tilda was moaning about not gettin' shushi stew. Us malts started to sing,

> *'I'm a Romani Rai, a true didikai,*
> *I build all my castles beneath the blue sky.*
> *I live in a tent, I don't pay no rent*
> *an' that's why they call me a Romani Rai.'*

As the men untied the 'orses, me and Ria cleared up the rubbish. I 'eard the gavver say, *'bleedin gypos.'* My Alfie called out, *'the gavvers are grunts, let's jel on, keep movin'.'*

We kept movin' but sometimes we stayed put for a while, like when we was 'op pickin' or pea pickin'.

> *'I'm a Romani Rom, I travel the drom.*
> *I hawk all the day and I dance through the night.*
> *I'll never grow rich, I was born in a ditch*
> *and that's why they call me a Romani Rai.'*

All together in the poove
the best of times.
Thank the blessed lord.

---

Poove – field; Chavvies – children; Mesci – tea; Vados – wagons; Dick-eye – look there; Gavvers – policeman; Malts – women; Yog – fire; Snoped – hit; Covels – belongings; Shushi – rabbit; Didikai – half Romany & half Gadje; Rai – a rough and ready person; Drom – road; Grunts – pigs; Jel on – let's go

# Hobben Time in the Hop Picking Days

When we were 'op pickin' the women would stop at four o'clock, go back to the vardos and get the yog goin'. We'd chop the vegetables and put everythin' in the pot ready for the guerros and the chavvies. We used to make Joey Gray. Slice the bacon, onions, plenty of 'tatas, fry in the pan on the yog with some gravy and salt. Everyone loved this 'obben, it warmed us up.

We'd eat together between five and six o'clock. There'd be a makeshift table set with the spoon, forks and washcloths, bowls of salt and pepper, baskets of bread. We'd sit around the yog with our plates on our laps. We always took our time, we'd finish every last bit on the plate. We chanked just enough to fill us up, no more, except when we 'ad shushi stew, we always 'ad more of that.

Once a week we'd bake an 'edghog, roll it in clay, bake it in the embers of the yog, leave it for a good while then break the clay open. The spines come away and what's left is the tenderest meat. The chavvies liked to watch this but there was always one who cried, feeling sorry for the little creature. Well we 'ad to eat. We used to bake a few at a time, as they're only small. Sometimes we'd put 'em in a zimmen and make a stew. We ate a lot of stew, especially if it was a cold or damp day. We ate well, that we did. We ate better than a lot of gadje's, see in the war time everyone was on rations. Us Romanies used to pick all our own vegetables in exchange for doin' a bit of work for the farmers. The men would bring 'ome the odd pheasant, we'd pick fresh 'erbs. We put anythin' we 'ad in the pot. We liked a lot of salt 'n'pepper. Kushti. Afterwards we drank strong mesci, none of this wishy washy stuff that they make nowdays, no, good strong mesci. I liked to put a drop of whiskey in it, a lot of us did, but there were a few who didn't touch the stuff. Me Aunt Louie wouldn't drink, she said it was the devil's brew and if yer drank, you'll go didilow.

*Hobben* – food; *Vardos* – wagons; *Yog* – fire; *Guerros* – men; *Chavvies* – children; *Chanked* – ate; *Zimmen* – pot; *Gadje's* – non-Romany; *Kushti* – very good; *Mesci* – tea; *Didilow* – crazy

# Somewhere in Apple Water Country

Me mum's cookin' shushi stew.
Me dad's chinnin' the koshties.
I'm practicin' handwritin' wiv a fine pencil.
I'm lookin' forward to sendin' a proper letter
To me cousin Louie, she's a didkai and goes
To school in London. Me dad calls it royal town
And says 'e wouldn't go there, not if yer paid 'im.
She 'as to wear a uniform, red and gold, but she
can't wear 'er gold 'oops, it's against the rules.
If I ever went to school, me dad would 'ave murder
If anyone touched me 'oops or me ears.

*Apple Water country* – a Romani term for the county of Herefordshire.
*Shushi* – rabbit; *Chinning the koshties* – making pegs; *Didikai* – half-Romany

# Just One Room

He stood on the back door-step,
took out a brand new key,
unlocked the blue door.

They both took their chockas off.
He walked in first, she followed.
Her eyes fell on the ceramic white sink
in the corner of the kitchen.

In the wagon they had four bowls;
one made of gold china for washing their bodies,
the others were metal:
one for pots and pans,
one for cutlery
and one for washing clothes.

The smell of fresh paint hung in the air.
Alfie knocked on the wall, stroked it,
took a deep breath.

Amy walked into the hallway,
neither spoke.
Once in the sitting room,
Amy's mouth opened, wide.

'Dikka kie Alf,'
He came to the door.
'We could fit our whole vardo in here,' she said.
'This is just one room.'

*Chockas* – shoes; *Dikka kie* – look here; *Vardo* – wagon

# The Gypsy Gift

Do you know someone who's got the gift ? I do, my Aunt Saforella. She was born wiv it and she knows everythin.' When she wakes up she knows what the weather's gonna be like and whose gonna be poppin in for tea, she'll say. *'Put the kettle on mum, our Evie's comin' over.'* My gran rolls 'er eyes and says, *'Who'd thought it, my child wiv the Gypsy gift?'*

Once a week, she yearns a few bob reading tea-leaves, she calls it dukkerin'. She makes the tea, sets the china cups on the table, puts bright red lipstick on and waits fer 'er first customer. She don't know it, but I've often sat under the table, 'oldin' me legs tight and listenin'. She puts on a posh voice and speaks very slowly and softly and I 'ave a job to keep quiet. She tells the folki all sorts of fings, like the type of mush they're gonna marry or 'ow many kids they'll 'ave. Once she told a woman that she was gonna come into a lot of money and the old dear jumped up and started runnin' around the room, shoutin *'I knew it, I knew it, me luck's gonna change.'*

At night when I'm in bed, I 'ear 'er makin' strange sounds, as if she's speakin' in a foreign language or perhaps stuck down a drainpipe. I 'ear granny callin' out. *'Go t'sleep Saforella, for cryin' out loud.'* In the mornin' I says to 'er, *'You don't 'alf make some funny sounds in your sleep, aunt Saforella.'* She puts 'er cup of mesci down and says, *'Oh, that's me speakin' in tongues, it comes on me now and again and I have to 'eed it.'* Well, me gran and me, we look at 'er and say, *'Dordi, dordi, that's the Gypsy gift for yer.'*

*Dukkering* – fortune telling; *Mush* – man; *Mesci* – tea; *Dordi, dordi* – dear, oh dear

# A Richooell

He has set aside a fine needle, a cork, a small bowl for the
panni which boils in the pot on the yog, some cloths and a little butter.
His baby chi plays with faidas, lining them up in a row.
He knows that in a short while she will holler then rove
but her sobs will die down and he would have done his job.

Just as his father did for his sister, he'll pierce her ears.
*'It's a richooell.'* He tells folk.
He picks her up, puts her on his wife's lap.
    *'Now 'old 'er tight.'*
The chi wriggles then settles.
He cleans both ears with the hot wet cloth,
puts pegs on both of them and as a lot of Romany men do,
he diddles.
    *'Diddley dee, diddley die, diddley, diddley, do.'*
He dips a needle threaded with cotton into the boiling pot,
removes one of the pegs and is eagle quick as he pushes
the needle through the lobe of the ear with the cork.

The chi screams.
He does the other ear.
The gold sleepers are put through both holes.
    *'There, there, my little chi.'*
His wife kisses the child as she sobs,
her small chest puffing up then down like a soft breeze.

Gently the father rubs butter on the ears.
He takes his hip flask out, unscrews the lid,
drops some whiskey onto his finger then rubs it into
the chi's mouth.
She screws her face up tight.
She looks at him.

    *'You'll thank me when you're older my gel.'*

---

*Panni* – water; *Yog* – fire; *Chi* – child; *Faidas* – pegs; *Rove* – weep

# Bones n' Spoons

before I played the spoons
I played the bones
before I played the bones
I listened
to me father
playing the spoons
to me granda
playing the bones
and as I tell you this
me son is listenin'
the bones, they are a waitin'
and the spoons, well they're in the kitchen drawer.

# The Plum Pudding Girl, a Little Gypsy Song

Phylly put your chockas on.
It's time to go to Shepperton,
to see yer gran and grandad
on a windy Friday night.

Plum pudden,
meat pudden,
bacon pudden,
suet pudden,
cooked in a cloth, tied with a string.

You'll 'ave to sing a song for them
and do a little dance for them
then they will blow the joter
when the 'obben's in the pot.

Plum pudden,
meat pudden,
bacon pudden,
suet pudden,
cooked in a cloth, steaming in the pot.

Phylly put your chockas on.
It's time to go to Shepperton,
For they will blow the joter
when the 'obben's kushti 'ot.

*Chockas* – shoes; *Joter* – whistle; *Obben* – food; *Kushti* – lovely

# I See You in the Hop Fields

*i.m. Phyllis Lane*

The Last Waltz by Engelbert Humperdinck
plays on the radio, a favourite of yours.
Whenever you heard it, you'd twirl around the room,
dipping here and there, the rest of us would groan,

*'Oh no, not Humperdinck again.'*

The green velvet chair that you used to sit on,
knitting one pearl, one plain is empty.
I see you in the hop fields,
you're hair tied up under a scarf,

your gold hooped earrings dangling.
You are picking hops, singing an old gillie,
perhaps 'I'm a Romany Rye?'
Walking back through the vines to the wagons,
your skirt swinging,

your father calls, *'Come on my Phylly, gel on.'*

You try to catch up with him.
I see you smiling.
I hear you say,
*'Daddy, daddy, wait for me.'*

*Gillie* – song; *Romany Rye* – Romany man; *Gel on* – come on

The author's grandfather,
Alfie Lane, mother Phyllis
and aunt Mary

Granny Amy
& Great Aunt Ria

The author's mum,
Phyllis

Harry Webb & cow

Mum Phyllis & Granny Amy

Gold earrings

Great Granny Amy Ripley (née Hoadley) with Great Aunt Vera and cousins Owen and Linda.
They are standing in front of the hop crib in Bishop's Frome, Herefordshire.

Uncle Tommy

Granny with her flowers

# Chickens in a Pen

They drove us off the tober,
we settled in a ken.
The chavies didn't like it,
like chickens in a pen.
They drove us off the tober
you've never seen the like.
We couldn't hear the cuckoo sing
or light the yog at night.
They drove us off the tober,
the politicians had their say.
We're Gypsies through and through.
Watch us rise and go our way.
They drove us off the tober,
we've settled in a ken.
The chavies, they don't like it,
like chickens in a pen.

*Tober* – road; *Ken* – house; *Chavies* – children; *Yog* – fire

# dirty little flower girl

us gypsy chavies 'ad it 'ard in the days when we 'ad to go to school. the gadjes used to call us names, they spat on us, told tales, but we were there to learn, it's what our mothers and fathers wanted. i'd rather 'ave been out on the tober, travelling around England, although i will say I'm pleased that I 'ad an education of sorts, it 'elped me to get on in life and I've 'ad some kushti jobs.

me sister and I went to the local school, we 'ad a lot of time off for travelling. I can't say that I liked it there; well I would 'ave done if we weren't all cooped up like chickens, sometimes I felt like I couldn't breathe. i didn't like mrs frances, me teacher, then again, she didn't like me. one lunchtime I was standing in the line waiting to get me 'obben, she shouted at me,

 *'You're holding the queue up, move along, be quick.'*

i moved along but i 'eard her say to another teacher,

 *'Dirty little flower girl.'*
somethin' snapped inside me 'ead and I said, without thinkin',

 *'I'm not dirty.'*

she looked at me, fierce like, her face turning red. she put 'er vast out, bent down and slapped me legs, 'ard. i didn't cry, just moved along the line to get me 'obben.

me dad picked me up from school, i was very quiet all the way home. Me mum gave me a cuddle and a kiss when we got in, she smelled of roses which was nice compared to the smell of steak and onions that she'd been cookin'. after dinner she undressed me to me vest and knickers, i sat on the draining board, as she started to wash me legs she called out.

 *''arry, come 'ere, dik at the baby's legs.'*

he asked me how I got the bruises, i wouldn't say. he said,

'*dordi, dordi 'as somebody snoped yer?*'
i cried but still didn't tell them. it was ages until I finally did.

the next morning me mum marched me to school. we went straight to the 'ead teacher's office. i 'ad to wait in the corridor, there was a strong smell of polish. i sat there for ages, i saw mrs frances go in, on the wall in front of me was a picture of the rounders team, i thought i'd like to be in that team, they all looked 'appy and friendly. after a while me teacher came out, walking fast, looking down at 'er feet. me mum came out. she grabbed me 'and took me to the classroom. she said,

'*it's done and sorted, now go and learn my babe.*'

i never did find out what 'appened in that office, i 'ad a good guess. i was at that school for another year but the teacher never bothered me again. i never did get to be in the rounders team though.

*Chavies* – children; *Gadjes* – non-Romany; *Tober* – road; *Kushti* – very good; *Dik* – look; *Dordi dordi* – Oh my goodness; *Snoped* – hit.

# In the Back Yard at Winslow Way

Granny's sitting in a deck chair. She's fanning herself with an old Spanish fan. She has a straw hat on and her cheeks are bright red. Behind her is a low whitewashed wall, beyond that the long garden full of fruit trees and vegetables.

*'Good God, its 'ot,'* she says.

She is wearing a pale pink dress with red polka dots on and a red and white pinafore. Her freckled bare legs stretch out in front of her. Her feet in sandals, her big toenails painted red. I'm playing with my doll Suzie who has real hair and pink lips, she is dressed in a bright orange dress, one that my Mum made.

My sister is lying flat on the ground. The tortoise is on her stomach, it's been there for ages. Yogi, our dog, is sitting next to her and is staring at the tortoise. Usually Bev is running around pretending to be a cowboy or playing with her cars, it seems strange for her to be so still.

Granny slurps her tea and says,

*'Ooh, that's a kushti cup of mesci, nice and strong.'*

I ask her why she drinks tea on such a hot day.

*'It cools the blood down, they all drink it in India.'*

I look back at the tortoise. He hasn't moved at all. My sister looks as if she's in a trance, as does the dog. I think I might give Suzie a bath, to cool her down. I ask Granny if I can use a bowl, she tells me there's one in the bathroom but I know that this is the one she uses to soak her feet so I tell her that I'll wash Suzie in the sink instead.

Soon after I've finished washing Suzie my Mum returns from her shopping trip. She tells my sister to get up off the ground but Bev says that she's waiting for the tortoise to reach her neck. I burst out laughing and one by one we all laugh. Suddenly the tortoise falls off of Bev's chest, he lands upsidedown with his stubby short legs sticking up in the air. Granny jumps up, says,

*'Oh, my lord, you've mullered it, quick pick it up.'*

Bev picks the tortoise up, runs down the garden to the long grass. She bends down. We wait and then a few moments later she calls out.

*'It's alright everybody, he's still alive.'*

I go inside, calm Suzie down and put her to bed. She's had enough excitement for one day.

*Kushti* – very good; *Mesci* – tea; *Mullered* – killed

# The Guveny — a haibun

Harry leans against the brick wall in the alleyway, smoking a roll-up. His black stadi pulled down, almost covering his right eye. He wears a navy and white pinstripe suit. Anyone would think he was off to the city, but no, he's taking five to prepare himself for the meeting with his parole officer. He's planning on getting there early and making a good impression.

Just as he's finishing his smoke a brown cow walks into the garden, eyes like coal, calm as you like. Harry looks up, wonders if he's dreaming.

> With nostrils flared
> breath rising into cold air,
> the brown cow bellows.

*'Well, I'll be blowed, it's a bloomin' guveney,'* he says.

A guerro runs down the road, stops at Harry's gate, shouts to another guerro who's marching briskly behind,

*'It's alright Jim, he's here.'*

Harry drops his cigarette butt, stamps on it with his right foot. He walks up to the cow.

*'Ain't you a kushti guveney? Where did you come from then?'*

The guerro tells him that the cow wandered off from the field near the reservoir.

*'We'll be getting him back now mate, sorry for any inconvenience.'*

Harry shrugs his shoulders, strokes the creature's head.

The cow stands erect
appears rooted to the spot,
oblivious to men.

Harry watches the men lead the animal away. He thinks this will be a good topic of conversation to share with his probation officer, keep the mood light.

*Guveney* – cow; *Stadi* – trilby hat; *Guerro* – man; *Kushti* – good

# Romanichals in the 1950s

(i)
covels packed
chavies scrubbed clean
me racklies bal washed with panni
the grai grizhomed holled


(ii)
opre and gel on
dikk the next atchin tan
a fellow chal pookers
kushti bokt

*Romanichals* – English Romanies; *Covels* – belongings; *Chavies* – children
*Racklies* – girls; *Grai* – horses; *Grizhomed* – groomed; *Holled* – fed

*Opre* – arise/forward; *Dikk* – look for; *Atchin tan* – stopping place
*Chal* – Travelling man; *Pookers* – calls out; *Kushti bok* – good luck

# The Greenhouse

Mourners spill out into the alleyway. Amidst the black are flashes of purple and red of women's scarves and men's ties.

My uncle, a staff sergeant in the army and just back from Germany, is dressed in his uniform. He leans against the kitchen wall, having a smoke. We drink tea laced with whiskey. My aunts dry their tears on freshly pressed white handkerchiefs.

I go into the sitting room and see my sister sitting on a stool, her hands clasped tightly on her lap. The coffin is open. Grandfather is in his best suit. His pocket watch hangs from his top pocket. A family photograph is tucked into his waistcoat close to his heart. His old hip flask lies at his side, no doubt there will be a little whiskey in there. He still wears his gold ring. He looks as if he's resting, as if he'll sit up at any moment. I place my hand gently on his ...

*Grandfather and I are walking down the path to the greenhouse. I am six years old. It's a hot day, I'm wearing my shorts. Weeds and wildflowers tickle my ankles. He pushes the door open, ushers me in, points upwards.*

*'What d'ya think of the grapes my gal?' Tilting my head back I see huge bunches, deep red, ready to be plucked. He reaches up, pulls a few down, rinses them in a bowl of water then places them in my hand. I bite one and the juice runs down my chin. I eat two more. 'They're lovely Grandfather.' He smiles, opens a can of beer, takes a mouthful and says, 'Do ya see these grapes? Do ya know why they're so tasty?' I shake my head. 'Well it's because the Mulo watches over 'em.' He laughs, I laugh but I'm not sure who the Mulo is.*

I finish my cup of tea and tell granny that I am going down to the greenhouse. The door is slightly ajar, the white paint faded, flaking. I push the door hard, go in and smell sawdust, stale beer and decay.

There is an open can of Pale Ale on the shelf, alongside three broken brown pots. An old knife with a blue handle, its blade stuck in the wood. It's the one he used to carve the wagons with. I bend down; pull an old crate out and in front of me the unfinished wagon. Taking a tissue from my pocket I wipe the dust off. It's painted red, green and yellow. Tiny faded net curtains hang limply against the small windows. The front door has minute horseshoes attached to it. All the Romanies believe them to bring good luck. I would love to have this wagon. Before I leave I look up to where the grapes used to grow in abundance. All that is left is a dried, tangled vine hanging loosely from the roof.

*Mulo* – spirit of the ancestors

# Pig's Trotters, Coronation Street
# and a Noisy House

It's 1963, I'm seven years old.
My sister and I are sitting on the floor
gnawing on pig's trotters.
The fire crackles and spits.
Coronation Street is on the dikkamengro,
Granny's going on about Annie Walker's hairstyle
and Bet's low-cut blouse.

>  *'Dordi Alf, dik at the raklies, they're like our lot in the beer shop.'*

She's standing in front of the mural,
a Spanish woman picking sunflowers.
It's like the one that Hilda Ogden has,
that's why Granny bought it.
She thinks there's a real Coronation Street somewhere.

>  *'I don't know why you have the box on when all you
do is talk, woman,'* Grandfather says.

Mum is on the old blue settee,
her legs curled under her,
lighting up a cigarette,
I cough and wave the smoke away, she tuts,
fiddles with her gold sovereign
which hangs on a chain around her neck.
She turns it over and over in her hand.

The dog barks,
the doorbell rings.
Granny shouts,

>  *'Oh, lummy, who can that be?'*
Grandfather says.
>    *'How do I know?'*

The dog barks,
the bell rings again and I think
why doesn't someone open the door?
The dikkamengro seems to have got louder.
The fire is roaring, I pull my cardigan off,
take my pig's trotter into the kitchen.

There is a man and two women at the door.
The man says they are Jehovah Witnesses,
I hear him saying that the world will end.
Grandfather tells him he's didilow and shoos him away.
I go into the hallway,
see my sister jumping onto Grandfather's back,
yelling yee hah.

I go upstairs,
lie on my bed, open an Enid Blyton book.

Just as I'm finishing the first paragraph I hear Granny saying,

'What's a Jehovah witness, Alf?'

He replies,

'I haven't got the faintest idea but they think the world's gonna end.'

'Oh good god,' Granny says.

Dikkamengro – television (looking box); Dordi – oh dear; Dik – look;
Racklies – non-Romani women; Didilow – acting strange/not with it

# Harvest Time in West Sussex

Wrapped up warm, holding onto mother's hands,
we kicked leaves as we walked down the old country lane
where hazelnuts grew in abundance.

Orchards of apples, pears and plums, ready for picking.

    *'Quick sharp, winter's coming,'* my Dad would say.

Scrambling up the ladder, reaching for the apples,
pulling them down, dropping them into the big basket,
we were quick as wildfire.

Plums, sometimes splitting in our hands.
We'd wipe them on our trousers and get told off by Grandma.

In the late afternoon, we'd stop.
We nibbled on sugar sandwiches, devoured the plums, sometimes
sipping Dad's cider, when he wasn't looking.

By the end of the season we'd be sick of the sight of apples
but the following year we were ready once again.

    *'It's a time of plenty,'* Dad used to say.

In the orchards we talked to the Gypsy boys.
They lived in painted wagons with shoulder-high wheels
and travelled all over the country.
They spoke in a strange language. We didn't understand any of it.

There was something about the Harvest moon,
the way it hung over our small village,
making night feel like day.

Back in our bedroom, gazing out of the window,
watching the smoke rise from the fires of the Gypsy camp
in a nearby field, we'd sip our cocoa.

'*Would you like to be a Gypsy George?*'
'*You bet, seeing different places, living in a wagon.*'
'*Yeah, me too. You know they eat hedgehogs?*'
'*No, I didn't, I don't fancy that, all those prickles.*'
'*Me neither.*'

We go to bed pig-tired, and even though the moon filled our room with light, once our heads hit the pillow, we'd be asleep before you could say, Jack-Robin.

# Lucy the Dukkerer, Epsom Downs

Rueben pulls the vardo up onto the grass verge, makes his mother some tea, gets a bowl of water for the Terrier Violet and helps his mother to settle on the blanket. He brings her to Epsom every year, his dad used to come too but since he lost the sight in his left eye, he likes to stay at home with the pigs and the pet goat called Horace. Lucy likes it when the sun shines as it does today, for her this means there'll be more customers. Someone calls out to her and she calls back, *'kushti divvus.'* She looks at all the Travellers, how well they're dressed and likes the fact that they always make an effort for Epsom. She's wearing her mauve velvet jacket with a red paisley dress, there's a pink carnation in her lapel. Her long hair is plaited and tied up on top of her head; it hasn't been cut in years. She's smoking her pipe just like her mother used to. She unwraps the dusty charms from an old cloth that she keeps in a deep pocket and places them in her red felt hat which lies upturned on the grass. A customer has come over and is now kneeling in front of her, fidgeting and yawning. Lucy takes the money, picks up the hat, shakes it hard then beckons for the woman to take one of the charms. This is done three times, the first represents the past, the second the future, the third the present. Each charm is turned over carefully in her hand before placing it on the bright red square of muslin that is on the blanket. She uses all sorts of charms to tell people's futures, tiny horseshoes, coins, crystals and even a variety of coloured buttons. *'The yoks tells me everythin.'* Lucy knows that the charms are just something to concentrate on. *'After all, I can't sit and dikk at someone's face for too long, can I?'*

*'Yer granny is worried fer yer, she's prayin' as 'ard as she can.'*

The woman begins to cry. Lucy speaks with with a quiet voice, her Welsh accent coming through. *'There now, my dear, you're blessed to 'ave 'er show up today. She says, you're a strong gel, you gotta leave that man, 'ee ain't no good for yer.'*

Lucy pauses, rubs her hands and says *'Yer need to see a doctor, yer granny thinks you might be with child.'* The woman's eyes widen as she looks down and mumbles. *'I don't know what to do.'* Lucy smiles softly, tells her to go back to her mother and that everything will work out. As the woman goes on her way, Violet jumps onto Lucy's lap and they both sit in the sunshine waiting for the next customer.

*Kushti divvus* – good day; *Yoks* – eyes

63

# A Romany Geurro Remembers

Facebook 27 December 2016

'i remember me uncle nassy lee living in a bow top vardo, it was on a grass verge in a lane called bonus lane in crewe he 'ad seven or eight children an' i used to visit wiv me other cousins bobby and taylor boy me uncle nassy was me granny's brother her maiden name was smith I'd love to 'ear from any of 'em. RT.'

Facebook 28 December 2016

'there was a traveller woman her name was sally lee she 'ad one eye and a son called money, she used to go 'awking with 'er trushnie filled wiv combs, pegs, old silver and lucky 'eather, i think she used to live around the pottery area of stoke – all the best.' RT.'

Facebook 30 December 2016

'it's nice to 'ear from you my gel – the 'op pickin' i done is at a place in hertfordshire called rimal – we used to stay in little cabins wiv straw on the floor that me mum made up into a bed, me dad was a pole puller he pulled the 'op vines down, we 'ad a crib and we used to strip the 'ops from the vine then put 'em all in the crib, you got paid by the bushel – a basket filled to the top worked out to a bushel, i used to go in the dryin' kilns, they dried the 'ops and they smelled of sulphur – it smelled strong – you mention rokkerin in romani, well apart from a few words I've long forgotten the language – me mum and dad spoke it all the time but since they passed none of us speak it i did 'ave a few pages of different words that me sister gave me but it's in a drawer somewhere. You're better to look on the internet i bet there's lots of sites where you'll find it – all the best. RT.'

*Geurro* – man; *Vardo* – wagon; *Hawking* – selling; *Trushnie* – hawking basket; *Rokkerin* – speaking; *Jib* – language

# Making the Vardos

*i.m. Alfie Lane*


Sitting on the doorstep
he picks up his churi,
makes the first cut into the oak,
the finest for small vardos.
He's taken to this since moving into the ken,
he's made one for two of his children,
now he's on the third.

The jook watches him as he carves the door,
he thinks of painting it red,
Mary's best colour.

He works quietly,
dropping the shavings into a bowl.
He remembers making the pegs,
Chinnin' the koshtie's, they called it
when he was on the drom.

The had always sold well,
The racklies used to say he was the best
peg maker in all of Kent,
he didn't like the fuss
but he was proud of what he did.

His dad taught him the craft,
how to grind the tips until they were sharp,
how to make the handle level so it fitted snug in the hand,
never scolding him if he got it wrong.

He rubs the tiny door down with sandpaper,
holds it up to the light,
brushes his fingers across it,

    *'Smooth as a pebble, eh Butch?'*

The jook barks. Alfie stops.
He yawns, the dog yawns.

> *'I'm tired, let's jell t'woodrus boy.'*

Tomorrow he'll paint the door.
When it dries he'll stencil on the drabos,
all in keeping.

> *'These little vardos are all we got now, eh Butch?'*

*Vardos* – Gypsy wagons; *Ken* – house; *Churi* – peg knife; *Jook* – dog;
*Chinning the koshties* – making the pegs; *Racklies* – women; *Jell t'woodrus*
– get to bed; *Drabos* – good luck charms/symbols

# Up Early, haibun

She walks the three mile journey in sun, rain and snow, pushing her empty barrow through the station yard. Burt the Guard is always there to greet her, he lost a hand in the trenches and she calls him a *'dear blessed man'*. Dressed in her green pinafore and coat, her side pocket tied around her waist, and wearing a green and purple head scarf, she sucks peppermints.

Pushing her barrow onto the ramp she enters the carriage at the end of the train, standing all the way from Feltham to Waterloo. Once there, she walks swiftly out of the station and over Waterloo Bridge then onto Nine Elms market where she buys the *'freshest, most colourful loolladi.'* This is where she uses cunning to get what she wants, never paying the full price. She bumps into *'all sorts of characters.'* There's Joey who runs the café, he gives her tips on the horses. There's old Mrs Kray who sells tulips when they're in season, a relative of sorts.

> Spanish dancers
> Blood orange dahlias
> soaking in water.

*'Ooh, yer can't beat 'em.'* She also loves carnations. *'ow much do yer want fer these cars'?* The seller says, *'Two pounds for you Amy.'* *'I'll give yer one pound fifty and not a penny more and I'll 'ave another two boxes.'* He tries charging her more but she's not having it. She walks away, he calls her back. *'Alright Amy, they're yours.'* The barrow is filled box by box. She ties them tight with string then says, *'I'm off 'ome.'* By the time she gets home to 'anarth, she's worn out. A bowl of oxtail, a drop of whiskey and she's ready for bed. Her husband wraps his arms around her waist. She says. *'Go to sleep Alf, I'm dukkered.'*

*Kushti* – very good; *Loolladi* – flowers; *Dukkered* – exhausted

# The Strawberry Gel

On warm summer nights they lay on thick blankets looking up at the stars. The door of the vardo left slightly open in case the chavies woke. They would whisper about the time they first met in the strawberry fields. He remembered the blue dress she used to wear, how her hair was braided on top of her head, her sovereign earrings unlike any he'd ever seen. She would tell him how she was taken by his honest brown eyes and the way he took her hand and said, *'Shall we go for a stroll Amy?'* He had picked a strawberry for her and it was the sweetest thing she had ever tasted. It was kushti bokt that both he and their gel had strawberry marks on their backs. They laughed at how she could never get enough of the fruit. They called her the strawberry gel. Their Phylly, with the corn coloured hair. He yawns loudly. *'Shush, go t'sleep Alf.'* They both settle down, his hand resting on her hip, her hand on his chest.

*Vardo* – wagon; *Chavies* – children; *Kushti Bokt* – Good Luck

# Strawberry Picking in Kent – Tanka

She's bent low, the sun full
on her back, red juice seeping
through sticky fingers.

When no one is watching, she pops a berry
into her mouth and savours childhood.

# The Table in the Hop Fields, Bishop's Frome, Shirley's Tale

We got to the 'op fields just as the sun was coming up. We walked across the poove and there was our Aunt Amy, pouring panni from the kettle into the big brown teapot. She'd covered the table with a white lace cloth and 'ad laid out 'er best china crockery.

*"Ere you are my gels, come and 'ave a bit of breakfast and a nice cup of mesci."*

Me sister and I couldn't 'elp but laugh, the table looked so funny in the middle of nowhere.

*'Now listen 'ere, we got a pick a lot of 'ops today, yearn ourselves some poshes.'*

We had to sit on a red checked blanket, the grass still wet from the morning dew. She gave us bread, cheese and a cup of sweet mesci. We looked up at all the 'obben that she'd prepared for the 'oppers. Plates of bread and ham, cheese, pickles and funny shaped biscuits. She put 'er 'ands on 'er 'ips and looked around as if she was waiting for someone.

*"ere 'ee is, 'bout time too.'* It was our Uncle Tommy, come all the way from Anarth, I knew wiv 'im 'elpin' we'd pick loads of 'ops.

'Ee came stridin' across the poove, a big smile on 'is face, 'is trilby on and 'is waistcoat all buttoned up, 'ee always did look smart.

*'Well well, ain't this kushti Amy? Yer made yerself 'at 'ome, I see. What a luvley spread.'*

*'It don't seem that long ago that we were on rations Tom, and you know me I do like a nice bit of grub.'*

'Ee kissed 'er cheek, bent down, tickled us gels and made us giggle. One by one the rest of our people joined us, wanting breakfast. They were just as amused at the sight of the table as me sister and me. We all knew that Aunt Amy liked to do 'er own thing, we never knew what the next thing might be.

*hungry finches*
*waiting for crumbs*
*as we ate our grub*
*a bell rings*
*it's hopping time*

*Poove* – field; *Panni* – water; *Mesci* – tea; *Poshes* – money; *Hobben* – food; *Kushti* – very nice.

# Wildflowers

She is tying bunches of wildflowers, placing them into a penerka, her arthritic hands working slowly. She stops, breathes in the fine fragrance, remembers the other flowers, some made of paper, for those she used a small peg knife to curl the petals, taking it up and over, one by one, taking time until they looked like the real thing. Then the small bunches of heather that she cut and put together in tissue paper with a thin piece of bass tied around the ends.

*She is walking with the vardos, holding the hands of her youngest children. Her husband is guiding the grai, she is singing an old song, 'I love to walk along the drom, in the month of May, kushti divvus, kushti divvus, it's a kushti day.'*

*She is in her vardo, birthing her fourth child, the one with the strawberry mark on her back. Great Aunt Carrie is bathing her forehead. After screaming and cursing, the welcome cries of her daughter, reminding her of the first flush of a mother's love.*

*Sitting on her dada's knee, singing a song about lollipops, her voice breaking as he bounces her up and down, his laughter mingling with hers.*

Now she lies on a hospital bed, her face chalk white, her eyes watering, her Granddaughter sitting close by on a hard backed chair, her fingers moving, like sea anemones, pushing, pulling, pushing, reaching out to her Granddaughter who is transfixed. *'Picking the flowers, smelling the scent, tying them up, two bob a bunch, kushti divvus, in the month of May.'*

---

*Penerka* — basket; *Vardos* — wagons; *Grai* — horse; *Drom* — road; *Kushti divvus* — a lovely day.

# Mother Courage in Feltham High Street

*Amy shuts the back door, takes off her boots, coat and money belt, picks up the photograph of her dead husband and wipes it with a clean handkerchief.*

What a day I've 'ad Alf, let me sit down and I'll tell you all about it. It was three o'clock and I'd just sold the last bunch of pink carnations. I packed up and pushed the barrow across the road. Well, what a sight. There were grown men shoutin', holdin' banners up 'igh. I've never seen anythin' like it. It was like the war, all over again. I kept going and then a policeman stopped me, I've met him before, nice man he is. He said,

*'You can't go across the square, there's a demonstration going on. It's the N. F. and they're getting a bit rowdy.'* Well Alf, I said,

*'Now look 'ere Sir, I'm a Romany woman and I've been sellin' flowers in this high street for nearly thirty years. I'm not lettin' any men get in my way.'*

I walked across that square, brisk like, with me 'ead 'eld high, whilst the guerros were shouting and staggering all over the place. One of 'em walked right up to me barrow and was lookin' in it. I called out, *'Keep movin.'*

When I got to the carpet shop, the man said, *'Come in Mrs Lane, sit yourself down. I'll make you a nice cup of tea. You're brave to walk across that square.'*

You used to know that man Alf, he lived along Snakey Lane years ago. Well, I needed the mesci, I was tremblin'. I said, *'do put some sugar in it. Oh, thank you and thank the Lord.'*

Well, I picked out a kushti blue carpet for the bedroom and I came out of the shop. Oh Alf, it was like a ghost town, there was no-one around. I pushed the barrow back across the square and went into Tesco's to get some 'obben for me dinner. Who should I bump into, my Raine, I told her all about it. She said,

'Oh Gran, you must be careful. You might have got hurt. A lot of people don't approve of the National Front.'

She told me all about 'em and I thought thank the blessed Lord they left when they did. Anyway I told her what I'd said to the policeman and she did laugh. She's like me that gel, strong and knows her own mind. Guess where she's takin' me next week? We're going to an Indian restaurant Alf and we're gonna 'ave a curry, a proper spicy one. I'm looking forward to it.

*Guerros* – men; *Mesci* – tea; *Kushti* – good; *Hobben* – food

# Mumpleys

sleepin' under trees or in bender 'uts, can't afford a vardo, some call us mumpleys, we're the gypsies that 'ide in the shadows, we don't know anythin', we 'ave to chore now and then, 'ow else do we get by?

me sister goes barefoot, her chockas wore right down, until the soles were flappin' when she walked, one day she tripped up, fell flat on 'er face.

*'throw those chockas away ryala, there's nuthin' wrong wiv goin' barefoot, the earth is warm and I'll lend yer me socks.'*

we laughed and then dug an 'ole, buried 'er chockas deep in the earth, that night we 'ad dandelion broth and the tastiest of bread, it 'ad been thrown out by the farmer's wife. we toasted it over the yog.

the next day we went out callin', got some kushti 'ole togs then sold 'em fer a few bob, we bought fish'n'chips, proper grub. we sat on a bench pookerin' about our 'ol dad, he used to sell scrap iron from an 'andcart, made 'is livin' from it. he 'ad a stammer, yer couldn't understand much of what 'ee was sayin' 'alf the time but 'ee 'ad a lovely way with the mouth organ, 'ee'd play it at night and 'ee always cooked us tatti-tatties and gave us apples. 'ee used to say, *'there ain't nuthin' wrong with bein' a mumpley, we're as good as anyone else, don't yer forget it.'*

---

*Mumpleys* – Not quite a true Gypsy but not a Gadje, living on the road; *Vardo* – Gypsy wagon; *Chore* – steal; *Chockas* – shoes; *Calling* – selling; *Pookering* – speaking

# Mother Remembers a Picnic in the Woods

The sun was shinin'. Me dad was up front carryin' the penerka with all the 'obben. Me mum was trailing behind with me aunts and uncles. I was 'oldin' me brother's 'and but he was a slow walker.

*'Come on now, little Alfie, we're gonna 'ave a kushti picnic.'*

Me dad found a big old Beech tree and put the penerka under it to keep the 'obben cool. Me aunt Vera laid out the blankets on the grass. Little Alfie jumped up in the air then fell down and stretched 'imself right out on the ground.

*''Ere, look at 'im,'* me Aunt said.
*''E's 'appy.'*
We all laughed.

Me and me cousins played ball then sat down to eat. We were lookin' forward to cold bacon puddin', chicken and pickles. I've never forgotten what 'appened next.

Great Uncle Joe came walkin' through the trees to where we sat. He was dressed in 'is best navy suit, 'is grey stadi and a red dicklo. Me dad said,

*'Where'd yer think you're going our Joe, to the Gold Cup at Cheltenham?'*

But we all knew the real reason 'e was dressed up, it was to see Carrie, 'is sweetheart, who was sittin' next to Great Granny. Uncle Joe turned as red as the pickled cabbage, I felt sorry for him. All afternoon 'e didn't leave Carrie's side.

He was my favourite uncle. He called me 'little turnip', on account that 'e always 'ad to pull me up onto the vardo. He made me laugh with 'is funny sayins, like *'close yer mooie, you'll catch bees'* and *'yer never know what's round the corner, waitin' to jump out'* then 'ee'd pretend to be a muller. After our 'obben we sang songs and grandfather played the mouth organ. Me great granfather 'ad too much parsnip wine and was fallin' all over the place.

*'Go and sit down dad, you're as drunk as a lord,'*
Me mum said.
*'Now what if I am skimmished, it don't matter?'*
Us chavies did laugh.

As we made our way 'ome I 'ad to 'old one of me grandfather's 'ands, whilst me cousin 'eld the other and we kept walkin' from side to side, zig zaggin' all the way 'ome to our vardo and laughing.

*'You two are didilow you are,'* 'ee said and that made us laugh all the more.

*Penerka* – basket; *Hobben* – food; *Stadi* – trilby hat; *Dicklow* – neckerchief; *Vardo* – wagon; *Mooie* – mouth; *Muller* – spirit or ghost; *Chavies* – children; *Didilo* – not with it

# Kamavtu

Mother was from Middlesex,
father, the Welsh Valleys.
He was a pole puller, she picked the hops.

One Friday night
under a sickle of moonlight
they sat on a bench
in front of the Green Dragon pub.

The landlord had filled an old bath with beer,
the hoppers were dipping their mugs into the frothy liquid,
which dripped onto their bare chests.

They were smiling as they wiped their mouths on the backs of their arms.

Father and mother sat quietly holding hands.
He leaned in close, was about to kiss her cheek
when a voice hollered from the darkness.

> *'Phylly, jel on, let's get back to the vardo.'*
> *'It's me dad,'* she said.

She jumped up, straightening her long skirt
then quickly turned and whispered.

> *'Kamavtu Jimmy.'*

He didn't know many Romany words but this one, well he just knew.

*Kamavtu* – I love you

# Two Brothers

Once a month Great Uncle Tom visits his brother Sam.
He takes a cab from Bedfont to 'Anarth, always.

'Alright Sam?'
'Alright Tom?'

Once inside he places a bottle of Paddy's on the table,
which is covered with a red check cloth, the one their mother made
when they were nippers.

He asks for a bottle of milk and two glasses.
The two brothers drink, first the whiskey, then the milk.

'That's kushti, that is Tom.'
'You can't beat a drop of Irish whiskey Sam.'

They mainly talk about horse racing and selling the loolladi,
but usually they sit quietly, drinking and thinking.

At half past nine or thereabouts,
Tom gets up to go, stretching his arms and rubbing his hands.

He leaves the bottle on the table.
There's always a drop left.

Sam picks up the bottle,
puts it in the cupboard.

'Goodnight Sam.'
'Goodnight boy.'

Tom goes straight home to bed, sleeps like a new-born.

Sam walks down the garden, picks some lavender,
breathes in its scent.

When he's lying in bed, he thinks about the whiskey,
how he's saved all the leftover drops,
pouring them carefully into one bottle.

Next month he'll surprise his brother.
He'll say, *'The drink's on me tonight Tom.'*

He goes to sleep with a smile on his face.

*Kushti* – very good; *Loolladi* – flowers.

# The Malvern Hills

Three weeks it took us to travel to to the 'ills in Worcestershire.
Malvern was the last atchin tan 'afore we settled in Bishop's Frome
for the 'oppin' season. We pulled up on the common, untied the grai,
got the yog going. The chavies were running around, 'appy as yer
like. The racklies saw to the 'obben and I liked to walk about and
look up to the 'ills, a kushti sight if ever there was one. Soon we'd go
to the spring in the bank and drink that pure panni. There was a gillie
we used to sing,

> *We've come this far, let's 'atch fer a while, dik at the kushti 'ills.*
> *We've come this far, let's 'ave some mesci, dik at the kushti 'ills.*
> *The panni runs a through it, the finest you'll ever taste,*
> *Grab the bottles, climb the slope, let's not time a waste.*
> *We've come this far, we're drunk on panni, dik at the kushti 'ills.*
> *We've come this far, we're ready for sov, dik at the kushti 'ills.*

There are some things in life that poshes can't buy, fresh pannis one
of 'em, but yer don't need me to tell yer that, or do yer?

*Atchin tan* – stopping place; *Grai* – horses; *Yog* – fire; *Chavies* – children; *Racklies* – women;
*Hobben* – food; *Kushti* – very good; *Gillie* – song; *Hatch* – stop; *Dik* – look; *Panni* – water;
*Sov* – sleep; *Poshes* – money

# Walking With the Wagons

*Leeks, spring greens, asparagus and onions, all to be picked.*

Heather on the common.
Yellow on the broom.
Walking with the wagons
on our way to Bishop's Frome.

The chavies they are laughin',
they saw a little dog.
He only 'ad three legs
but was dancin' wiv a frog.

Stopped to 'ave some 'obben,
we sat around the yog,
thinkin' back to 'oppin' days
when racklies sold the togs.

Heather on the common.
Yellow on the broom.
Walking with the wagons
On our way to Bishop's Frome.

As we near our atchin tan.
The women shout 'hooray'.
We unpack all our covels
then untie the grai.

We've come to pick the leeks
and yearn a nice few bob.
We'll see our Gypsy frenos
and find an extra job.

Heather on the common.
Yellow on the broom.
Walking with the wagons
on our way to Bishop's Frome.

We've travelled all of England.
Not knowing what's ahead.
And in this kushti wagon,
is where we lay our 'ead.

The Gypsy life's the best,
We roam the pooves and droms.
You'll never see us glum.
We've fire in our bones.

Heather on the common.
Yellow on the broom.
Walking with our wagons
On our way to Bishop's Frome.

*Chavies* – children; *Hobben* – food; *Racklies* – women; *Togs* – clothes; *Atchin tan* – stopping place; *covels* – belongings; *Grai* – horses; *Frenos* – friends. *Kushti* – lovely; *Pooves* – fields; *Droms* – roads

NOTE: Bishop's Frome in Herefordshire where the Romany travellers used to pick hops every year

# Safe in Our Vardo Tonight, a lullaby

I'll gather you into my arms.
Keep you safe from harm.
We'll sit by the yog and I'll rock you 'til sov.
Safe in our vardo tonight.

    Safe in our vardo tonight.
    Inside the candles alight.
    For here we'll lie, my little chi.
    Safe in our vardo tonight.

I'll gather you into my arms.
Keep you safe from harm.
We'll wait for daddy, my sweet chavi.
Safe in our vardo tonight.

    Safe in our vardo tonight.
    Inside the candles alight.
    For here, we'll lie, my little chi.
    Safe in our vardo tonight.
    (repeat)

*Yog* - fire; *Sov* – sleep; *Vardo* – wagon; *Chi* – baby; *Chavi* – child

# The Lungo Drom

Bare, blistered feet.

She walked
over stone
on grass
through thicket and brush
in water,
snow,
flowers and mud.

Her hair grew long,
flowing like a river.
Tiny silvery fish latching
onto each tendril,
longing for the open sea.

At night
she slept in bushes, caves, beside trees.
She dreamt of fire.

She drank from streams,
picked heather, lavender rosemary for healing,
exchanged them for bread,
kept on walking.

Her hair turned white.
Her bones thinned.
Her body bent over
and her eyes grew weak.
Still she kept on moving.

One early morning under a mottled sky
she stopped.
The moon shone in her body.
Light fell on the ground
and she knew
this was her atchin tan.

*The lungo drom* – the long road;  *Atchin tan* – stopping place

# Kushti Grai

*i.m. Michael Edward O'Neil and the horse known as Mad Alf*

He was called Mad Alf, on account of 'im bein' on the nervous side. He couldn't stand still, 'cause of the shell-shock see, all the noise of the guns, did 'is 'ead in. Me da bought 'im fer a shillin', otherwise it would've bin the knacker's yard, like so many others. 'Ee was an army grai, a kushti grai.

Me da thought the world of 'im and took 'im everywhere. The chavies loved 'im and 'ee them. The only time 'ee stood still was when they were strokin' 'im. *'Ain't you a luvley boy?'* they'd say. Me da sold 'errins in the main square and Mad Alf would trot to and fro until it was time to go 'ome. I was only a nipper but I remember it well. Me da comin' back to the vardo, tellin' us about 'is day, stinkin' of fish.

'Ee used to let me give Mad Alf some 'obben, carrots and grains and all the time 'ee kept 'oppin' from one foot to the other, 'ee was beautiful though. When we settled fer the raddi, we'd 'ear a strange noise, a sort of screechin' sound, 'igh pitched. Da said *"Ee's 'ad it 'ard, 'ee done 'is bit.'* *"Ee must of bin frit to death, going didilow on the battlefield,'* me da said, then 'ee tutted and put 'is 'ead down so I couldn't see the tears.

One day I 'eard someone cryin', I went outside and saw me dad on the ground, is 'ead bent down, one vast on the grai's neck, the 'uver on 'is back. Mad Alf lie mullered. The first time I ever saw a mullered grai. No words fer it.

Da made a wooden carvin' of Mad Alf which took pride of place on the mantlepiece. 'Ee couldn't spell but 'ee managed to write, *'Ere is Mad Alf, our phral, a kushti grai. Duvel Parik me freno.'*

*Kushti* – lovely; *Grai* – horse; *Chavies* – children; *Vardo* – wagon; *Hobben* – food; *Raddi* – night; *Didilow* – out of his mind; *Vast* – hand; *Mullered* – dead; *Phral* – brother/best mate; *Duvel parik me freno* – God bless my friend

(With sincere thanks to Charles O'Neil, who kindly allowed me to write about his Grandfather Michael Edward O'Neil who lived in Carlisle and bought the horse known as Mad Alf).

# The Boshamengro – The Gypsy Fiddle Player

*(Birkenau concentration camp, 1944)*

Handcrafted from spruce and maple,
the fingerboard of black ebony
was once finely polished.

The Gypsy would tuck the fiddle under his chin,
pick up the bow and play,
stamping on the ground.

He kept it with him as long as he could.
He noticed scratches, dents,
but he held it close, like his own child.

On a cold dark morning
he is ordered to get up,
and follow the line.
With little time,
he draws himself up,
takes the fiddle in its old black case,
places it against the wall, whispers, *'Parruka tute me freno.'*

As he joins the line, he remembers when he was a boy,
taking the fiddle from his father's hands,
his heart plucking fast,
as – it – is – now.

*Parruka tute me freno* – Thank you my friend

February 1943: At Auschwitz-Birkenau, a family Gypsy camp was set up in a wooden barracks. August 2 1944: Over 4,000 Roma and Sinti men, women and children were murdered in the gas chambers. January 27 1945 at 3pm, Soviet soldiers reached the camp and found only one Rom among the survivors.

*"Except for a few survivors, a whole people unique in its life-style, language, culture and art, was wiped off the face of the earth. The death of the Gypsy Nation was more than physical; it was total oblivion."*

AZRIEL EISENBERG, Witness to the Holocaust, 1981 (New York).
Taken from Da*nger, Educated Gypsy, Selected Essays* by Ian Hancock

# The Gypsy Camp at Auschwitz

*the branches on the trees bend and sway*
*leaves fall and settle on the ground*
*sunlight seeps through mottled clouds*
*and all is quiet*

*a woman with long red hair*
*picks a blade of grass*
*holds it up to the light*
*remembering her husband*
*the shape of his mouth*
*how he spoke her name, Narilla*

*men kek bissa: we will not forget*

*an old chal with silver hair*
*takes his hat off, feels the warmth of the sun*
*on his head*
*his chavo was four years old when they were imprisoned*
*a year later he was taken and was never seen again*
*he had dark curls and hazel eyes*

*a chavali runs into the arms of her mother*
*who remembers she once had twelve chavies*
*all had hair the colour of the darkest earth*
*and eyes like wolves*

*men kek bissa: we will not forget*

*winter birds mourning on the branches*
*the earth remembering*
*how it has given refuge to the dead*

*no longer dead leaves trampled underfoot*
*they have become wild breathing flowers*
*growing in the dust.*

*Men kek bissa* — we will not forget; *Chal* — man; *Chavo* — boy; *Chavali* — girl; *Chavies* — children

# Acknowledgments

Huge thanks to the editors of the following journals, websites and magazines in which these poems have previously been published: *Poetry Ireland Review*, 2018; *Poethead Women's Poetry Platform*, 2019; *Under the Radar*, Nine Arches Press, 2020: *The Clearing*, Little Toller Press, 2019/20; *The Narrow Road Journal*, 2019; *Vox Galvia*, The Galway Advertiser, 2020; *The Blue Nib,* Issue 43, 2021; *The Travellers Times*, 2019/20/21; *The Poetry & Jazz Café Magazine* — Festival of Chichester, 2017/18/20/21; *Writing in a Woman's Voice*, 2020/21; *Poems and Pictures* — Mary Evans, 2021; *Fevers of the Mind Digest*, 2020; *One Hand Clapping*, 2021; *Bonnie and Crew*, 2019; *Foxglove Journal*, 2019; *Ink Pantry*, 2018; *The Ofi Press*, 2020; *Romany Routes — the Journal for The Romany & Traveller Family History Society*, 2018/19/20/21; *Word City Lit*, 2020; *Fresh Air Poetry*, 2019; *Mookychick*, 2020; *Skylight 47*, 2021; *Dodging the Rain*, 2019; *Places of Poetry*, 2020; *Impspired*, 2020/21; *Words for the Wild*, 2020/21; *Live Encounters*, Winter 2020; *Contemporary Haibun Online*, 2019; *Here Comes Everyone*, Rituals Edition, 2019; *Wild Women Press,*2021.

Thanks also to the editors of the following anthologies in which some of these poems have appeared: *Gifts of Gravity and Light*, Hodder & Stoughton, 2020; *The Unicorn Poetry Anthology*, Acteon Press, 2020; *Scratch of the Hop*, Logaston Press, 2020; *Witches, Warriors, Workers*, Culture Matters, 2020; *Persona Non Grata*, Fly on the Wall Press, 2018.

"The Lungo Drom" was awarded the Moon Prize for outstanding writing in 2020 with *Writing in a Woman's Voice*.

"The Greenhouse" was performed at the *Poetry Ireland Review* 40th Birthday Celebration in Dublin in 2018.

"A Memory of the Hop Fields" was featured in the film, *Stories from the Hop Yards*, made by Catcher Media for Herefordshire Life through a Lens Project in 2018. The same poem was made into a short film by the Wellington Primary School for the same project in 2018.

Many of the poems in this collection have been performed at the following festivals: Ledbury Poetry Festival; Chichester Festival; Blakefest; Winchester Poetry Festival and South Downs Poetry Festival.

# In Appreciation

I would like to thank the following people for their support and encouragement: my husband Simon who is always there for me; my son Luke and daughter Rebecca for their support and generosity; my cousins Julie Morgan and Shirley Rees for their input into our family history; my ancestors who inspire me daily; Mike Doherty, editor at the *Travellers Times* and Isaac Blake at Romani Arts for their support; James Simpson, my mentor and friend; Hannah Brockbank and Brenda Bayne for their friendship and generosity; Barry Smith for giving me some wonderful opportunities; Mark Davidson at Hedgehog Poetry Press for being so gracious and for publishing my first pamphlet; Christine Rowlands for her friendship; another cousin Tara Sutherland who has done extensive research into the Ripley family; Rita Ann Higgins, Chris Murray, Angela France and Jess Smith for their wonderful endorsements; to all the friends and colleagues that have been there for me; thank you Siobhán Hutson for all your hard work; for designing the cover and helping my book come to life. And last but certainly not least a huge thank you to the amazing Jessie Lendennie for publishing this, my first full collection, and for her input, guidance and kindness. I am eternally grateful.

RAINE GEOGHEGAN, MA, is of mixed heritage, English, Romany (Romanichal), Welsh and Irish. She is a performance poet, prose writer, playwright, voice over artist and performance skills coach. Prior to writing she was a professional actor, dancer and theatre practitioner. She trained in dance, theatre and drama therapy. She founded Earthworks, a Women's Theatre Collective in 1993. Illness and disability brought her to writing. Her poems and prose have appeared in journals, magazines and online. Raine's work can also be found on YouTube and Sound Cloud. Her work has also been widely anthologised. Nominated twice for the Pushcart Prize; Forward Prize and Best of the Net, she won the Moon Prize for Writing in a Woman's Voice and her poem "The Birth of Rage" was Highly Commended in the Winchester Poetry Competition for the 'Reaching Out' category. Her three pamphlets, *Apple Water: Povel Panni*, *they lit fires: lenti hatch o yog* and *The Stone Sleep* are published with Hedgehog Poetry Press. *Apple Water: Povel Panni* was chosen as a Poetry Book Society 2019 Selected Pamphlet. She is the Romani Script Consultant for the musical *For Tonight* which will be performed in the UK and the USA in the near future. She is featured as the 12th Profile for the Romani Cultural and Arts Company and was Headline Poet for the World Storytelling Café in 2021. Her video was viewed over 2500 times. Her play *The Tree Woman* was performed online for the worldwide Earthquake Festival in October 2020 with the San Francisco Theatre Collective. She was a Guest Poet at Over the Edge Poetry event in Galway in 2020 and has performed at many other poetry events in Ireland and the UK. In February 2022 she participated in *A Suitcase of Poetry*, an Irish project founded by Fiona Bolger and Viviana Florentino and culminating in a video on YouTube. In 2024, Raine will edit an anthology of Romany women writers and artists, to be published by Salmon Poetry.

# salmonpoetry

Cliffs of Moher, County Clare, Ireland

*"Publishing the finest Irish and international literature."*
Michael D. Higgins, President of Ireland